Father Myself

Father Myself

James McDermott

Nine
Arches
Press

Father Myself
James McDermott

ISBN: 978-1-916760-10-3
eISBN: 978-1-916760-11-0

First published February 2025 by:

Nine Arches Press
Studio 221, Zellig
Gibb Street, Deritend
Birmingham
B9 4AA
United Kingdom

www.ninearchespress.com

Printed in the United Kingdom on recycled paper by:
Imprint Digital

Nine Arches Press is supported using public funding
by Arts Council England.

Supported using public funding by
ARTS COUNCIL
ENGLAND

dedicated to the memory of my father Shaun McDermott
who died aged sixty from COVID-19

Contents

Admission

the night of January 7th you leave
your bedroom door open as if
to let something in or out you
try to blaspheme and choke your way to sleep
but rasping breath like fireplace bellows
continuous thunder cough keeps us all
awake at three Mum flies from spare double
to call *the meat wagon* after five days
begging warning you *this isn't man flu*
tonight you don't object curled up foetal
white hot hacking up yellow green black phlegm
lips blue septic skin mottled like corned beef
shaking I wait outside your room as two
medics affix oxygen mask to your face
stats should be one hundred they're sixty-six
but you're sixty I'm only twenty-eight
hypoxia asks for an ice lolly
Mum begs me *fetch Twister from the deep freeze*
cold as a morgue you suck it like a thumb
when you can eat no more you dribble *done*
your feet are helped into *Nandad* slippers
draped in black dressing gown I watch all this
reflected in glass of a framed photo
our family hanging on the landing
you're shuffled past me splutter *see you Jim*
I cry *take care of yourself* you descend
the stairs to a stretcher they belt you in
to a twenty-one-day roller coaster
to Norfolk and Norwich who bell at six
he's COVID positive fifty fifty

Dog and Bone

I thumb a text concerning you going
to ICU   copy   paste it   send it
to friends   is it too sore   laborious
to scratch it out seventy times   or just
the modern world   duplicating terror
reducing blood and guts to emojis

*

Mum's mate collects your phone charger
to drive it to the ward so you can keep
talking to us   a conduit of life
to help the dog and bone survive

*

in cold grey living room   Mum and I try
to ring your Nokia   you don't pick up
Mum mouths *he might be on oxygen*
as we listen to the dialling tone
beep like an ECG monitor   I
sweat one day soon your lungs might not answer
nurse could make the call to disconnect you
never again will I give you three rings
to let you know I'm home   never again
will *Dad* appear on the vibrating black
mirror of my screen   your phone will be
returned to us   little carbon coffin

Oh Father

oh father   what were you thinking
those ninety-six hours sixty years long

on your belly   in bleached ICU bed
like a beached seal gasping for breath   as blue

nail bombs shatter your lungs   did you kick
yourself for not swallowing three needles

did you find God   pray turn water into
antibodies   or pine for the coffin

did you regret fag butts   handcuffs   Christmas
ache for your teddy bear Seamus   Grace's

school shoes   two wedding cakes   a retirement
caravan in Cromer with *Tid*   or did

you shadow box   mother   sister in law
Jim   Luke   Mary   waiting   for the trip gong

Fight

when you yank off your oxygen mask   I
beg you *keep fighting Dad*   as if

I'm proud parent cheering you at sports day
do you find my calls help your breath sprint on

or do my yelps make your face flush   eyes sting
like mine did age seven when you shouted

at me from sidelines   to *run like other
lads* could   I couldn't   no matter how hard

I cried   strong mind wouldn't beat weak body
I stop wailing at you   replace the mask

to hold your hand in mine   as cold and thin
as gold medal   neither of us could win

Ventilator

Wednesday January 12th four a.m. when
steroid you vibrates under Mum's pillow
the doctors have fucked off   come take me home
your Manc bleeds in to Norwich nurse   *hello*
Shaun's pulled off his oxygen   he's going
to be ventilated   Mum sobs   *see you*
soon Bubs   this isn't goodbye   it's goodnight
the line goes dead as artificial air
keeps sedate you conscious   but Mum and I
cannot be put to sleep   we're loaded
waiting to shoot to ICU   we live
in the wings of dress rehearsal grief
as we're retold you're *critically stable*

Poirot

when Dad is ventilated   Mum and I
kill nights in the living room binge-watching
Suchet's Poirot   but why   my blood used to
come together for it like Sunday roast
in 2006   when Mum's mind broke
she read all the Christies   maps back to her
little grey cells   we're going through murder
Hercule always makes sense of death   it's just
pretend   the corpse is really Toby Jones
who wipes off blue make-up and lives somewhere
down South after the director shouts *cut*

Patient Board

father   you never saw this patient board
wipe-clean white-board easeled at the end of
your bed   your adult life blu-tacked to it
wedding photo   your Dad's too-big grey suit
holding Mum's off-white charity shop frock
a school photo of me   age five   Luke   three
both pudding bowl haircuts   your gummy grin
a professional portrait of Grace
cream cardy   beaming moon face   butterfly
clips in chocolate locks   snap of Poppy
piglet snoozing on Luke's chest   your second
granddaughter born ten days before you die
on this ventilator   you   Mum   Luke   caught
grinning as you open our vintage shop
we'll have to empty next Sunday   in black
marker   *your nurse today is called Sarah*
Mary James and Luke are visiting
at 1 o'clock   you're in a safe place Shaun

13.58, January 28th

I never planned to be at your death bed
so soon   but here we are   face masked   cracked glass

of untouched water   a wobbly stool   I
cool beside your white hot bedsheets   your face

a hog's   your snout dribbling tubing   your tongue
a red apple   doctors turned you over

praying for a new leaf   to drain fluid
on lungs   but they couldn't   so here I am

you were there when I cried into the world
it's fair I see you out   nurse says *it's time*

to slide out snotty lines   vacuum bloody
phlegm from your mouth   turn off support and I

cling to your arm like a cliff edge then death
makes a Bacon painting of your boy's face

Family Room

small grey family room   Mum Luke and I
wait on three ripped leather-clad chairs   a nurse
Sarah shuffles in with a bag for life
of framed photos from Dad's bedside   wedding
graduations   birthdays   our childhood breaks
Jack Wills sports bag stuffed with clothes Dad came in
blue jeans   black dressing gown   *Nandad* slippers
Sarah perches on rickety table
to give my Mum a small white business card
this is the bereavement office number
there's no rush but they're open nine to five
call to collect his rings   necklace   ear stud
then she hands us each a little orange
knitted heart in a plastic bag   a note
inside that says *together we will beat*
COVID   Sarah smiles   *a little something*
to remember him by   right then   see you

COVID-19 Grief Symptoms and What To Do

a found poem using text from the NHS website

Symptoms can include:

a high temperature or shivering (chills)
a new, continuous sob – this means sobbing a lot for more
than an hour, or 3 or more sobbing episodes in 24 hours
a loss or change to your sense of future
shortness of breath
feeling tired or existential
an aching brain
a sore soul
a blocked or runny self
loss of hope
diarrhoea
feeling sick or being lost

What to do if you have symptoms of grief:

Try to stay at home and avoid contact with other people

You can go back to normal activities when you feel better

Fit as a Fiddle

the bespectacled Crocs-wearing surgeon
calls with the cause of death *COVID chronic
obstructive pulmonary disease* you
had narrowed inflamed tar-scarred lungs sixty
ciggies a day twelve to fifty you were
never diagnosed as often breathless
wheezing chest-infected you refused to see
the quack because of balls biceps clenched fists
you should have been shielding first in the queue
for three pricks of Moderna not *whittling*
about side effects read in rags boasting
I'm fit as a fiddle your strings have snapped
your neck was trached your body ventilated
now your song's stopped and I hear violins

Mispronounced

you were always Missus Malaprop
mispronouncing chimney *chimley* you smoked
your lungs to ash   bottle *bockle* you wined
away lock-downs   mental *menkal* you thought
vaccines ridiculous   *ridiclious*
but now father   you are pronounced dead   *dead*

Chapel of Rest

we appear in the chapel of rest   next
door to travel agents   Chinese   florists
to be found by bow-tie wearing usher   who
walks us like black hang-dogs to cloud white door
opened to candle lit box room   small oak
table   Bible   two chairs   a catafalque
draped in cream sheets   a gran's sunken body
I'm told is my father's   *he's here*
he isn't   he is   covered waist down
in soil brown quilt   wedding shirt ironed
by Mum two days before   moleskin waistcoat
both back-cut like hospital gowns to slide
over rigor mortised arms   greyed blonde hair
blow-dried to quiff   deep tissue injury
from proning scabbing your forehead   swollen
cheeks rouged   like mine aged twelve when you lost me
in Mum's make-up   called me *sissy*   your lips
Botoxed with cotton wool   your eyes sewn shut
to sobbing folks who your death happens to
who see your left ear once pierced by a needle
wondering why you wouldn't have three more

Little Monuments

Dad's pierced left ear lobe
I touched for the first

and last time in the chapel of rest
to see this monument never noticed

before   to recall its exact thickness
precise pinkness   the depth of the puncture

Solid Liquid Gas

at Burnham Staithe   I welly-shuffle on

February's black ice   will March melt it

make it evaporate   twelve again

Mister Leckey's lab   *solid*   *liquid*   *gas*

my Dad   flesh   blood   thin air   pre-grief time was

concrete   but now   Dalí   melting clocks   smoke

Portrait of My Father Without a Face

on a coat hanger   I drape your yellow green
        striped shirt   wrap it in brown Barbour jacket

to its hem   I staple the waist of your
        blue denim jeans then bulldog clip brown brogues

to cuffs   I hang you out on rotary
        clothes line   watch wind make circling ghost of you

Black Wheelbarrow

Dad's black wheelbarrow still
leans against his creosoted *man cave*

both handlebar ends capped with one of his
threadbare hose-green gardening gloves

looks like a big-gutted bloke with his hands up
as if backed against the shed at knifepoint

a man falling   leaping   sinking
or Dad   waving

Photographic Memory

both in black jeans   blue shirts   arms draped round one
another's shoulders as we grin at dusk
on Weybourne's pebble beach that orange June
is my favourite photo I have with you
father   I can't recall what we did   said
that day   I just remember this image
where now we lie in long-gone time
buried in this six by four inch casket

Waiting on the Hearse

you sped from here in a red ambulance
rasping *I will come home* a long black snake
your hearse slides in our drive king-sized to ward
death bed to pine coffin to clock you shrunk
to bone lilies Mum reduced to vintage
dark hat your youngest son a bruise-blue suit
and the congregation jaundiced with shock
all greyer than your blood but why friends last
saw you as a Santa hat not black phlegm
blue lips ventilator embalmed tortoise
they don't know of Pinot handcuffs tossed coins
do pennies drop for them that dropped for us
five weeks ago we are all lit fuses
Mum and I sob as the partners grip hands

Carbon Copy

at father's funeral   his glum old gang
hold my eye   hand   a beat too long   do they

watch for sobs or are my peepers carbon
copies of Dad's   twin chin   clone lips   ghost nose

'He's in a Better Place'

where is better than Holt tiny tearooms
antiques emporiums are you scoffing

fruit scones in creamy Cromer caffs skinny
dipping in Sheringham sea wind-swept

on Holkham beach if you are no longer
in our cottage are you in Felbrigg Hall

Windsor Castle up the Eiffel Disney
roller-coasting camping in the Hanging

Gardens punting skiing cruising Soho
Castro slut-dropping in Heaven being

papped by Warhol shooting Cybermen
are you TARDIS travelling through time space

Dadmin

a found poem from a conversation with my mother

Aviva kept me on hold for thirty
are that many people really calling
about life insurance   suppose we are
in a pandemic   if we're all dropping
who's got half hour to spare   they won't tell me
the figure over the phone   they'll post it
should be here in three to five working days
they need his death certificate today
your Dad's medical records   which takes 'em
two to twelve weeks to read so they can find
reasons not to cough up when I have to
shell out for skips   coffins   if I don't get
the policy I've paid for   I'll kill him
that money   it's a thank you   a sorry

Fridge

I open the cooler and hear my Dad
call out to Mum   *he's in the fridge again*

on his second supper   from the front room
she would snigger   as I'd sneak down   Dad would

sneak in for Secretary Bird   creep up
behind me to make our nightly in-joke

we'd smirk   not finding it funny so much
as familiar   but now   when I open

the ice chest   I don't hear him   I see him
in rotten apples   liver pâté   red steak

Robbed

your youngest Luke says you *were robbed from us*
as if two green paramedics broke in
shoved an oxygen hood over your *bonce*
bundled you into the back of screaming
ambulance   if you were robbed   were you
complicit in the theft   letting death in
by not triple locking your blood because
I'm scared   the side effects might hurt my heart
'cause of my atrial fibrillation
and both my folks' tickers stopped at my age
was it dangerous driving of your body
whilst under the influence of tabloids
even though *ball and chain* was *out pricking*
assault   on souls who drowned in that first wave
who would've rushed for your life raft   surgeons
on fire who slaved to save them   a kind
of suicide   poisoning Christmas puds   birthday buffets
my wedding cake

Super Spreader

the outbreak of grief
the infection   the fever   the shakes   the choking
the lock-down of grief
the stay home   the self-isolation   the incubation period
the shielding   the social distancing of grief   the two metres
the can't hug   the herd immunity   the super-spreader
the daily bulletin of grief   the face covering   the tiers
the handwash   the bleach   the work from home of grief
the remote worker   the essential worker   the frontline worker
the ventilator   the you're on mute of grief   the bad signal
the trouble connecting   the sorry I'm late   the zoom bomb
the invisible plague of grief   the negative   the positive
the self-testing   the WHO
the personal protective equipment of grief
the two walks a day   the baking   the gardening
the reading   the roadmap to recovery of grief
the adapt and overcome   the endless reinfection   the new variant
the new normal

To Have the Virus that Killed my Father

when my lateral flow shows two blue lines   I'm faint
to shoulder parasite that set father's
face on fire   burnt him alive   stamped out
his lungs   each time I cough I sweat thought of
ventilators   even though I'm water
not wine   passion fruit not couch potato
twenty-eight not sixty-a-day   the sighs
when I'm one blue line   virus passing
through my body   lightly   as if a ghost

Alive

you turn to ash   I turn to nuts   bottom-
less espressos   collagen enemas
bananas   broccoli   blueberries   grapes
become stomach crunches   star jumps   squat thrusts
a skipping rope   swap Bakerloo line for
Reeboks   to crawl with my four-year-old niece
felt-tip our lips bright red   paint on tattoos
jump in muddy puddles   swing through the trees
duckwalk   dip   spin with bears   be animal
on the dance floor   you animated meat
I hug my flesh   hold this body I am

Shauny Bubble

I clock you in Nivea pink lather
as I soap your granddaughter's little limbs
like you scrubbed mine when I was *muddy knees*

I clock you in seafoam on Weybourne beach
strolls we never did together   I clock
you rise in lager pints we never shared

I clock you erupt in boiling water
as I stir two a.m. tea in your *Best*
Dad mug   I clock you trapped in a spirit
level still reminding me I'm not straight

I never asked you why *Shauny Bubble*
was your life-long nickname   maybe *Bubble*
was your first word   your first teddy   maybe
everybody knew you'd float briefly   burst

So Long

when I outgrew your cradle arms
when I got too grand to stand on your shoulders

when I chose Mum's Posh over your Becks
when I swapped you for RuPaul   Stephen Fry

when I slung my hook to grammar   lectures
when I head for boys   hardbacks   matinees

when I howled *I'm a fag* and you burnt me
when your pissed fists were cuffed on Christmas Eve

I couldn't cry *so long* at your death bed
but I've waved bye to you so many times

Father Myself

falling trapdoor belly tasered but not
bed bound banshee clutching rosary
aching for Happy Meals jam sponge Yule logs
did I tsunami sob myself for three
weeks when you were machine now bone dry sand
bury our heads in verse   clenched fists   bombshell
made me bastard   Mum black latrodectus
karma for your being needless sleeping
beauty Poppy can't kiss Nandad awake
maybe *fairy* kicked off grieving thirteen
opened closet had to father myself

Play Small

I told myself that when you died   I would
be reborn taller in pink stilettos
they say *time heels*   free from tension   I'd let
my wrists go limp   unzip bruised lips   rouge them
uncork my throat to gush glitter   semen
vogue to Todrick Hall songs in the kitchen
without my face catching fire when you
swagger in and throw me a scathing stare
that pulls a trigger   makes me six again
caught in Mum's red pumps in your gun-point eyes
nails felt-tipped pink pretending I'm Baby
Spice screaming *Who Do You Think You Are*
who will I be brave enough to be now
I don't need your approval   now the first
source of my blush is no longer flesh   blood
maybe nothing will change   my idea
of you   of what you thought of my queerness
will squat in my head like it always did
when you were alive making me play small

Words Inside Father

heart hater after earth
hear fret fear ·fare
fate raft heft heat
eat tea her era
he er ha ta

Louder Than Words

the night before I leave home for uni
you shout me downstairs to *front room* I find

Buddha belly in armchair parapet
your right fist full with five twenty-pound notes

you can't hold my eye but hold my left hand
to pass the gift a lone tear drops from you

a penny plopped into a wishing well
I know this deed is your way of saying

goodbye good luck take care so I fill up
nod thanks fearing to hug would shake us both

like piggy banks broken now at your grave
I stand by you still stony faced to voice

goodbye good luck take care we didn't say
too much father like gods we spoke through acts

Dead Time

dear God
Buddha Gilgamesh karma fate whatever
please please gift me back the time when father
picked me up from Sibsey school
in his blue Vauxhall Corsa
dropped me at Cromer station
to commute to Norwich Theatre   my partner
all that dead time silent   he knew
nothing of dialogue   catharsis

Clearing Your Chest

I box up beta blockers from your chest
of drawers   dentures   knee brace   Nicorette gum

three unopened letters from Doctor Clark
imploring you to have Pfizer vaccines

school photo of you   twelve   eyes blue from belt
of father   mother   brothers   their orders

of service   portraits of you cradling Luke
me   floating Mum on your wedding day   snaps

of bro bearing two kids   me hugging books
Mum jiving with girlfriends   unused condoms

no coins   passport   lottery ticket   torch
I throw in your towel   wonder if you did

Mug

every morning you'd wake father   first thing
brew a *cuppa   proper milk   two sugars*

to slurp it on cream settee in the snug
spy crows dig graves with beaks in back garden

every morning I stir   first thing   recall
you've evaporated   no lips to slurp

no body to hydrate   grief has made me
mug with hole in   people expect me to

function even though I can't   I'm leaking
they won't chuck me nor let me bin myself

I just have *to learn to live with the hole*
to be half full   hold less but carry more

Grief Work

but I've done my grief work   sobbing over
photos   nappies   school shoes   suncream   crackers
in your armchair   brogues   bingeing your beloved
soaps   cheese and onion crisps   hairs from your comb
built a new home from pens   cocktails   yoga
climbed all five rungs on the ladder   screamed *no*
for thirteen weeks   punched God before begging
if I become straight will you resurrect
my Dad   won't respond   I shrank to black lab
who can't leave his basket until the egg
timer accepts the sun rises and dies
daily   I'm still axolotl who can't
grow back its spine   aching to know how long
will I grieve my father   is the answer
how long will he be dead and me alive
isn't to live to grieve   people ageing
changing irreversibly every day
every second passing a little loss

Lucky

over Guinness   my best mate sighs
we are lucky   we both have a family
death out the way   right now we've only one
loss each to grieve   but soon   our Mums   partners
our mates   ourselves   might lose our eyes   ears   minds
our memories of milk   Jäger   champagne
soon   our bodies will have to bear the weight
of their bodies   soon   our bodies will be
graveyards   we order another Guinness

Taxidermied Sloth

at Cambridge Museum of Zoology   we sip
oat lattes underneath a fin whale skeleton

twenty-one metres long   eighty tonnes
the weight of eight double-decker buses

are these the dimensions of today's ache
for you on this first anniversary

I look to encased taxidermied sloth
I blink and it becomes you embalmed

I wish I'd kept you
the sharpest edge is knowledge that I will

never see your body   knowing I can't
learn the backs of your unseen knees   you aren't

on the planet somewhere   you are extinct
the stuffed sloth turns to a mirror   has loss

drained me   skinned me   froze me   posed me
to make me look like I am still alive

Measuring the Year Since You Went

dadmin   death certificates   empty chests
well-thumbed family snaps   bin bags   bonfires
sobbing buckets   clenched fists   Temazepam
sleepwalks through High Kelling woodland
to spy a fawn witness a road-killed stag
then skip away in chase of mates   leaves   light
pints of pale ale in coastal pubs with pals
who hand me their grief stories like Kleenex
chain-reading Elly Griffiths crime thrillers
to see Ruth Galloway decipher death
books of grief poems
making mirrors of them   open windows
ten Bics bleeding two-hundred elegies
on to notepaper bandages   questions
questions   *how do I get re-lost in the*
texture of days   how do I live as boys
books   bricks I sweat for outlive me   how do
I love   those I kiss will become corpses
mantras   *live the life he gave you   life is*
too short to mope   people projects presence
gym membership   two hundred cheeseburgers
sixty concerts with Mum before she's dust
dates with daddies   teaching children to write
like you taught me   driving myself
hugging myself   as if I've learnt
how to become my own father

James

age six   James means Bond   cars   guns   but I am
silver Spice Girls Heelies   pink nails   I say

my name already knowing it's a punch
line   I'm sixteen   my father is boiling

a kettle by closed window when I tell
him   I am gay   he turns his back on me

as if I am the past   I'm twenty-six
in the living room   drunk on New Year's   Dad

queries if I'm dating someone   my heart
full hot kettle   I grill if he recalls

turning his back on me   and then he spills
he had a brother named James   who was bi

in eighties Manchester   my father was
the only man James told before he took

his life   James comes from Hebrew name Jacob
which means to supplant   to take the place of

Last Words

I watch from the threshold of my childhood
bedroom as two medics shuffle your black
dressing gowned body past me   under your
oxygen mask   dry cracked lips dribble   *see
you Jim*   your body's last words to mine   Jim
your nickname for me since birth   *see you Jim*
as if you're saying goodbye to my child-
hood self   as if Jim's about to die or
Dad   did you mean *I see you Jim*   as now
choking for life   you know Jim's queer childhood
your rainbow son you once denied   father
was this acceptance of me   finally

I watch from the doorway of the living
room as Mum phones your voice in I
CU   I breathe   *hello Dad*   your voice cries
hello James   your voice's last words to mine
before the ventilator is switched off
Jim dead   resurrected as James   adult
name everyone calls this human   your last
word to me father was *hello*   as if
in death you learn rainbows are tricks of light
you   me   we're blood   bodies   voices   as if
at death   you meet me for the first and last time

Acknowledgements

'Admission' was first published in *Shooter Literary Journal*.

'Dog & Bone' and 'Poirot' were first published in *Dreich Magazine*.

'Ventilator', 'Family Room', 'Alive' and 'Lucky' were first published in *Lighthouse Journal*.

'Fight' and 'Patient Board' were first published in *Atrium*.

'13.58, January 28th' was first published in *Southword*.

'COVID-19 Grief Symptoms and What To Do' is a found poem using text from the NHS website.

'Fit as a Fiddle' and 'Robbed' were first published in *Poetry Wales*.

'Little Monuments' and 'Virus' were first published in *Ink, Sweat & Tears*.

'Shauny Bubble' was first published in *The Alchemy Spoon*.

'Father Myself' and 'Play Small' were first published in *Queerlings*.

'Louder Than Words' was first published in *Magma*.

'Grief Work' was first published in the Pilot Press anthology 'Responses To *Love's Work* (1995) by Gillian Rose'.

'Clearing Your Chest' was first published in *Off The Chest Anthology*.

'James' was first published in *The Cardiff Review* and selected for The Best Of The Net Anthology 2024.

Thanks

Thanks to these publications and their editors for seeing something in my poems and for giving them homes.

Thanks to Jane Commane for editing and publishing this collection with such characteristic care.

Thanks to Richard Scott for mentoring me through the writing and redrafting of several poems in this collection.

Thanks to Ian Humphreys, Paul Stephenson, Joelle Taylor and Luke Wright for writing endorsements for this book.

Thanks to my family for your continual love and for allowing me to write about such a personal, painful chapter in our lives.

Thanks to the staff of Norfolk and Norwich Hospital for the care they gave my father during his terminal illness in the pandemic.

Thanks to friends Mark, Jeni, David, Dawn, Ollie, Janie, Raymond, Simone, Marcus, Pasco and Lucy for your friendship and support during my grieving process and during the writing of this collection.

Thanks to my partner Aaron for your heart, mind, playfulness, patience, encouragement, coffee, home-cooked dinners and cuddles.

Thanks to my father, for bringing me into the world and for teaching me to read and write. We loved each other quietly, clumsily and judgementally but we loved each other. This collection is for you.